Best from G-Man

BATMAN ®

IN *Detective* COMICS ®

FEATURING THE COMPLETE COVERS OF THE SECOND 25 YEARS

VOLUME 2

ABBEVILLE PRESS • PUBLISHERS
NEW YORK • LONDON • PARIS

Editors: Amy Handy (Abbeville) and Steven Korté (DC Comics)

Front cover: *Detective Comics* No. 600; May 1989.
Back cover: *Detective Comics* No. 566; September 1986.
Frontispiece: Detail of *Detective Comics* No. 561; April 1986.

Covers reproduced in this volume were provided from the collection of Joe Desris. All cover credits researched and assembled by Joe Desris.

Captions note the pencil artists, followed by the ink artists, as could best be determined; however, this list may not be definitive. While the authors have endeavored to identify all of the artists involved, they apologize to any person misidentified and invite such person to inform them of the error.

Library of Congress Cataloging-in-Publication Data
(Revised for vol. 2)

Batman in detective comics.
    Vol. 2 has subtitle: featuring the complete covers of the second 25 years.
    Includes indexes.
    1. Batman (Comic strip)   2. Comic book covers—United States.
PN6728.B36B4 1993   741.5'973   93-22768
  ISBN 1-55859-643-7 (v. 1)
  ISBN 1-55859-837-5 (v. 2)

INTRODUCTION
by Joe Desris

Master detective, or archcriminals' pawn? Cold-blooded destroyer, or hot-blooded romantic? Bane of chaos, or fallen idol? City savior, or brooding menace?

From hapless victim to heroic vanquisher, Batman has witnessed—and embodied—the entire spectrum of law and order and its opposing side. He has been turned into a bronze statue, a genie, and a scarecrow. He has been imprisoned in a block of ice, a wall of flame, and a giant robot brain. He has been attacked by aliens, ghosts, vampires, wild animals, and his own Batmobile. He has stalked enemies alone by night and has fought crime as part of the "Batman Family." He has appeared to split with Robin several times and even seemingly murdered him. He has been assassinated himself on numerous occasions. And along the way his physique, attire, enemies, cohorts, indeed his entire image have evolved. But over half a century of tinkering has not diminished his resiliency or popularity. In fact, the Dark Knight commands more worldwide recognition today than ever before.

Encompassing issues 301 to 600 (March 1962 to May 1989), this volume reproduces the second set of three hundred covers from *Detective Comics,* the flagship title of publisher DC Comics and the first magazine to feature the adventures of Batman. Created by artist Bob Kane, the Masked Manhunter debuted in issue 27

(May 1939), and after only eight appearances had usurped the regular cover position.

According to the comic-book chronicles, a very young Bruce Wayne experienced the trauma of seeing his parents murdered. Over a fifteen-year stretch, the orphaned Wayne developed his crime-fighting abilities, becoming adept at acrobatics, boxing, science, and detective skills, which he combined with an overwhelming sense of honesty and justice. When a bat flew into the Wayne Manor study one evening, Wayne found the omen he needed to embark on his crime-fighting career as the Batman, a relentless and potentially lethal fighting machine (although his own personal code of ethics forbids the taking of human life). An unequaled tactician and strategist, he is gifted with vast knowledge, unlimited resources, finely tuned skills, and powerful determination. Though he possesses no traditional superpowers like X-ray vision or the ability to fly, the Dark Knight is nevertheless a true super-hero: a virtually unconquerable opponent.

A six-year period of tremendous change and of exponential growth in popularity for the Gotham Guardian began late in 1963. A change of creative staff ushered in a new approach to the character to celebrate Batman's twenty-fifth anniversary. Sheldon Moldoff, who had been working as a ghost artist for Kane since July 1953, produced his last *Detective Comics* cover for issue 326. Julius Schwartz—who followed Jack Schiff as editor—brought with him a new team of artists and writers, most notably Carmine Infantino, who introduced a more angular and graphic style to the series.

The new staff was responsible for shaping the "new look," as heralded on cover 327. Because of his success in revamping other classic DC characters—including the Flash and Green Lantern—Schwartz was given virtually free rein and was responsible for numerous innovations. He heightened Batman's detective skills, developed new villains, introduced new logos, changed the insignia on Batman's costume, and placed an elevator in the Batcave. He bumped off Alfred (actually, the faithful butler gave his life to save Batman's) and brought in the overprotective, middle-aged Aunt Harriet in order to have a female presence at Wayne Manor. (He named Aunt Harriet after a character in Hoagy Carmichael's song "Rockin' Chair.")

In short, Schwartz introduced a vastly different Batman. At first reluctant to take the job because "it meant having to read up on the subject and everything that went along with it," Schwartz finally agreed after some urging from the DC brass. But he did overlook a few important details early on: "In the first Batman story I plotted, I pulled two boners." First, Batman operated by daylight, which of course was inappropriate for a crime fighter who had built his reputation on chasing villains by night. Second, Batman held the villains at bay with a gun, even though his own solemn edict against killing precluded him from using such a weapon. (The Dark Knight was, however, uncharacteristically armed for a very brief time early in his career. This was chronicled in the "Year Two" storyline in issues 575–78.)

Dramatic, exciting covers undoubtedly help sell magazines,

but arriving at a cover idea can be a tough assignment. At the same time, covers must stop short of revealing *too* much of what awaits readers inside. Schwartz always worked closely with his staff to arrive at cover and story concepts. (His likeness was even incorporated into covers, as on 453.)

The covers in this volume reflect a wide array of storytelling techniques, ranging from the outright silliness of an alien zoo (cover 326) to the agony of Batman's tarnished reputation (cover 330), and even to what appears to be his ultimate defeat (covers 366 and 528).

Cover 320 spotlights Batman and Robin as an odd pair of mummy manhunters. "We've . . . both turned completely green!" exclaimed an emerald-hued Bruce Wayne to a lime-colored Dick Grayson after they had been exposed to an exploding disc inside an alien space capsule. Wanting to protect their secret identities, they became bandage-swathed heroes until both were back in the pink. Another unusual situation arose on cover 340, as they battled a mysterious villain named the Outsider. Able to animate objects and have them attack the Dynamic Duo, this villain somehow managed to make the Batmobile come alive; the car reared up like a titanic metal panther, ready to pounce on its owners. It even chased them up a wall!

Batman vanquished? Unlikely, yet possible. But actually dead? The Dark Knight does indeed appear to be deceased—or nearly so—on a number of covers (360, 427, 469, and 586, for example). The stories always turned out to have another explanation, such as an imaginary event (cover 347) or a hallucination (cover 524).

Another unique cover device was the recurring gorilla motif (covers 339, 482, and 562). Dating back to the 1950s, the use of gorillas on the covers of various DC Comics titles for some reason captured reader attention and significantly increased sales for those issues. The gorilla covers "sold like crazy," affirmed former business manager Irwin Donenfeld. "We had a gorilla doing various things in all the titles and every time we did it, it worked."

A new element of cover detailing was attempted on covers 348 to 365 (1966–67). Known as Go-Go Checks, the checkerboard pattern that ran across the top of every issue for a year and a half was not simply a reflection of the era's pop-art movement. Since some newsstand racks displayed comics vertically, revealing only the upper portion of a book, the pattern was intended to make DC's comics stand out and thus, theoretically, increase sales. "What a ridiculous thing," Carmine Infantino declared. "It was the stupidest idea we ever heard because the books were bad in those days and that just showed people right off what *not* to buy." But Donenfeld disagreed: "I was trying to find a way of making DC Comics pop out on the newsstand. It wasn't a bad idea; it just didn't work the way I wanted it to. It didn't add anything, but I thought it might." In fact, total sales for the entire DC line during this period were at their peak for the 1960s, sales for Batman-related titles increased dramatically, and DC was outselling all of its competitors. The checks were most likely cancelled as a waste of precious cover space, and interestingly, sales did begin to stall about a year later.

Editor Schwartz also trotted out new backup heroes. The first of these was Elongated Man, the stretchy sleuth who teamed with Batman in book-length adventures on several occasions (covers 331 and 343). Over the years, other heroes such as Hawkman, the Human Target, the Atom, Jason Bard, Tim Trench, and Green Arrow served as a bunch of second bananas to Batman's lead. Their adventures were an important element in this title's detective-style storytelling tradition, but there was never any doubt about who the star was. Issues 454–80 are actually touted as *Batman's Detective Comics,* and even the few covers completely devoid of Batman's image (516, 521, 544, 557, and 581) still include him in the logo.

Covers 481 to 492 trumpet the appearance of the entire Batman Family: particularly Alfred, Batgirl, Commissioner Gordon, Bat-Mite, Man-Bat, and the most obvious supporting-cast member—Dick Grayson, a.k.a. Robin. Created in 1940, ostensibly as someone with whom younger readers could identify, the Boy Wonder was originally intended to provide additional plot material, while his character proved a convenient device to enable Batman to carry on dialog. Significantly, Robin was the comics' first superhero boy sidekick, soon followed by many imitators, both successful and forgotten.

Batman's Rogues Gallery of course continued in full force, as Schwartz and his staff mined the classic archenemies. "That I decided to do right off the bat," jokes Schwartz. "I simply returned to the ones Schiff had been neglecting to use in the past: Joker, Catwoman, Penguin." As with the first 300 covers of *Detective Comics,* the Joker was once again the most frequently spotlighted villain. The Grim Jester's green hair, chalk-white face, and hideous grin resulted from swimming in a catch basin of chemical wastes. During his first two years of comic-book chronicles, the Clown Prince of Crime often left a Joker playing card at the scene of a crime. His victims wore a grisly Jokeresque grin thanks to the villain's most dangerous weapon, Joker venom, which produced almost instantaneous death. Arrogance, absurdity, and maniacal laughter became other trademarks of Batman's most famous foe.

The most memorable type of bad guy on these covers is the villain with a gimmick, not just a pug in a dark suit brandishing a revolver. The hideously scarred Two-Face, whose half-destroyed visage echoes his split personality, is a master criminal obsessed with the number two and the concept of duality, basing his crimes on these themes (cover 513). Catwoman, undoubtedly the most formidable female opponent, brandishes a cat-o'-nine-tails and specializes in crimes revolving around feline motifs (cover 570). The Scarecrow, formerly a professor of psychology and now a professional criminal, uses drugs and other methods to induce fear in his victims and delights in studying its effects (cover 571). The eccentric Mad Hatter plots to control his victim's minds (cover 510) or delivers a deadly hat attack (cover 573). In addition to these classic creeps, other nefarious felons were featured, including Birdmaster (cover 348), Black Mask (cover 553), Corrosive Man (cover 588), Manikin (cover 506), Ratcatcher (cover 586), and Squid (cover 524).

In 1965, Schwartz and his crew unearthed one villain unseen since 1948: the Riddler. The alter ego of Edward Nigma ("E. Nigma"), the Riddler had no special powers but was a master criminal strategist who loved to drop clues hinting at future felonies. The Riddler also had the honor of becoming Batman's very first TV foe. When the premiere episode of the new *Batman* TV series aired on January 12, 1966, it was the Prince of Puzzlers who was gleefully trying to outwit Batman and Robin. Not bad for a guy who had been missing in action for eighteen years.

To say Batman's newest incarnation took the nation by storm is an understatement. The show was an instant hit, elevating the Gotham Guardian to overnight media sensation. Initially broadcast twice a week, the *Batman* series was the ultimate in campy satire, full of intentionally corny dialog, deliberate overacting, and ubiquitous Bat-gizmos. The series also boasted handsome production values and chic pop-art design. Even the fight scenes had style, as giant animated sound effects like "KAPOW" or "KLONK" filled the screen. Adam West played it relatively straight in the title role, but he was surrounded by scenery-chewing villains and a pun-spinning Boy Wonder. In the first episode, Robin exclaimed, "Holy ashtray!" setting a pattern for the rest of the series, with phrases as diverse as "Holy Human Surfboard!" and "Holy Oleo!"

William Dozier, executive producer of the TV series, did not follow comics, which probably explains how a comparatively obscure villain like the Riddler, with only three published appearances, was chosen for the series pilot. Lorenzo Semple, Jr., wrote the screenplay for the first two-parter and developed the TV series bible. He also adapted several Batman comic-book adventures for TV episodes.

Many elements from the comics—including the major characters and their motivations, the secret identities, the Batmobile, Gotham City, and Wayne Manor—found their way to the TV screen, where they were joined by such innovations as new villains, new friends (Police Chief O'Hara, for instance), and an expanded role for Aunt Harriet. Chronically befuddled by the sudden departure of Bruce Wayne and Dick Grayson on yet another bird-watching or fishing expedition, the slightly dim Aunt Harriet appeared frequently during the show's first two seasons. According to Dozier, making her a prominent fixture around Wayne Manor served to quell occasional public speculation about a homosexual relationship between the Dynamic Duo. Almost from the beginning, Dozier wanted more women introduced. Before the series even aired, he declared in a letter to Semple, "Let's remember we must work dames into these scripts, both for Batman and Robin, wherever feasible."

Some of those "dames" turned out to be villainesses and molls, but perhaps the most memorable woman on the series (next to Catwoman) was Batgirl. The original comic-book Bat-Girl first appeared in 1961 as teenager Betty Kane, niece of wealthy heiress Kathy Kane, who was secretly Batwoman (cover 302). When the TV series proved to be a hit, DC Comics decided to re-model the character to attract some of the female audience the show had generated. On cover 359, Schwartz showcased a brand-new Batgirl, and her success eventually garnered her co-star status beginning on cover 384. The alter ego of Barbara Gordon, the commissioner's daughter, Batgirl was to become a major player in the third season of the TV series.

Much of the TV show's general direction was essentially the unacknowledged work of Batman's co-creator and first writer, Bill Finger. It was he who had originally scripted all those over-sized props and inescapable death traps, as well as Robin's penchant for bad puns, a quarter-century before they found their way onto the television screen. The death-trap device in particular became a staple of the TV series, serving as an ideal bridge between two-part episodes.

As Batman triumphed on TV, he found his way into newspapers, magazines, a feature film, a syndicated newspaper strip, and, two years later, a Saturday morning animated series. Sales of Batman comic books skyrocketed, and Bob Kane even began to exhibit paintings in galleries. The show also inspired an insatiable market for Batman paraphernalia. Millions of dollars' worth of worldwide merchandising descended on the public to fill a sudden demand for Batman lunch boxes, telephones, night-lights, belt buckles, bedspreads, and Pez dispensers, to name just a few items.

The Caped Crusader seemed to be turning up everywhere in 1966, even on his own jars of peanut butter and jelly.

Despite its popularity, the televised version had little impact on the comic book, although the publishers did capitalize on the show's success on covers 353–65 by substantially reducing the *Detective Comics* logo to make room for a new Batman logo. Batman also gained additional exposure on many other DC covers, ranging from enlarged logos to more frequent and more prominent appearances in other titles. At Irwin Donenfeld's suggestion, faithful butler Alfred had been included in the TV series and was therefore resurrected in the comics. But overall, the television incarnation of Batman fostered an image vastly different from that found in print. Revered by some fans and despised by others, the *Batman* TV show was nevertheless responsible for making the Caped Crusader an immensely well known and recognizable character, proving once again that comic-book heroes could be tremendously successful outside their native medium.

Having made Batman a household name, the series concluded in 1968. "Not bad for what was essentially a novelty show," producer Dozier remarked at the time. "In the last rating, the show was still leading in its time period. But adults had wearied of the series, and the audience had become more and more juvenile. The kids don't care if it's a repeat. So why go on spending $87,000 for new ones?"

Not all comic-book fans, however, had been fond of the televised Batman. In comic-book letters columns, some had derided the show's irreverence from the outset. A significant change in direction in the comics manifested itself in 1967, when artist Neal Adams's first work on Batman appeared. His realistic style and dramatic composition quickly reconfigured the post–TV era Gotham detective, generating enthusiastic fan response. In the early 1970s, Adams, along with inker Dick Giordano and writer Dennis O'Neil, made Batman once again a creature of the night. Metaphorically, the young man who had stood over his parents' grave vowing to bring villains to justice had returned.

Other changes were in the air. Dick Grayson left for Hudson University (issue 393), effectively splitting the Dynamic Duo until school vacations. Simultaneously, Bruce Wayne shut down the Batcave and Wayne Manor, packed up his gear, and moved into the Wayne Foundation building, located in Gotham City. While Robin more frequently battled campus crooks, he still occasionally returned to Gotham to combat crime with his mentor.

Dick Grayson was among the teen heroes who formed the first version of the Teen Titans, which eventually disbanded as solo adventures and schooling demanded more of their time. As he matured, Grayson decided that he had outgrown his earlier image; his goals and attitudes had become markedly different from those of a more obsessed Dark Knight. The Boy Wonder had become the Teen Wonder. Grayson subsequently became the super-hero Nightwing, turning the guise of Robin over to junior high school student Jason Todd. When Todd, who first appeared as Robin in issue 526, lost his parents in their battle with Killer

Croc, the youngster had a motivation for vengeance, and Bruce Wayne had a new ward.

By 1982, Bruce Wayne had returned to the rural Wayne Manor, and Batman was again working out of his true home, the original Batcave. A real turning point for the Gotham Guardian came in 1986, when Frank Miller's critically acclaimed four-part graphic novel *Batman: The Dark Knight* was first published. A creative and commercial success, it garnered unanticipated world-wide press coverage for Miller, DC Comics, and Batman. Set in a depressingly bleak near-future, the series established fashionably darker tones for Batman that remain in vogue today. "For me, Batman was never funny," Miller wrote in *Batman: Year One.* "I was eight years old when I picked up an 80-page annual from the shelf of a local supermarket. The artwork on one story looked good and scary. Gotham City was cold shafts of concrete lit by cold moonlight, windswept and bottomless, fading to a cloud bank of city lights, a wet, white mist, miles below me."

Dennis O'Neil became editor effective with issue 568 and brought Batman still closer to his roots as a mysterious gothic avenger. In O'Neil's view, Batman was a man whose life was completely shattered by the murder of his parents, and that terrible event shaped his persona into "something both more and less than human." This was a crime fighter "driven, tormented, obsessed, as dark in his way as the mean streets he prowls." Though the inescapable doom trap and life-threatening danger lurking behind every door have always been part of the Batman mythos, many more images surfaced throughout the 1980s of an especially bruised and battered Batman, defeat apparently inevitable (covers 528, 586, and 597, for example). According to O'Neil, Batman demonstrates that "evil always produces a counterforce and that humanity and compassion can survive the worst ugliness."

Also of note are covers 598–600, the three-part "Blind Justice" saga written by Sam Hamm, who co-wrote on the screenplay of director Tim Burton's outrageously successful 1989 feature film *Batman*. From architecture and lighting to costumes and plot, the movie also mirrored the darker mood of Miller's opus. From the somber 1970s creature of the night to the gritty Dark Knight motif of the 1980s, the imagery surrounding the Gotham Guardian has become even darker and more atmospheric, perhaps reflecting the bleaker realities of modern crime and justice.

As this collection makes evident, changes, modifications, and new stories are a way of life for Batman. He survives, as he has for over fifty years, in spite of his evolving image, or perhaps because of it. Imagine Batman without Robin, without a Batmobile, a Batcave, his vast array of gadgets, or even without his Rogues Gallery. All are now integral to Batman storytelling and all became significant milestones, yet none existed at his inception. Surely Batman's future will accommodate more fantastic felons, surprising new equipment, and secret nocturnal prowls. No matter who is chronicling his adventures, the Gotham Guardian will always be assured of steady work in his hometown.

ROGUES GALLERY

LIST OF ARTISTS

MARCH 1962; NO. 301
Cover artist: Sheldon Moldoff

MAY 1962; NO. 303
Cover artist: Sheldon Moldoff

JULY 1962: NO. 305
Cover artist: Sheldon Moldoff

AUGUST 1962; NO. 306
Cover artist: Sheldon Moldoff

SEPTEMBER 1962; NO. 307

Cover artists: Dick Dillin, Sheldon Moldoff

OCTOBER 1962; NO. 308
Cover artists: Dick Dillin, Sheldon Moldoff

DECEMBER 1962; NO. 310
Cover artist: Sheldon Moldoff

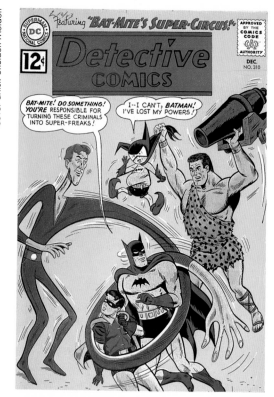

JANUARY 1963; NO. 311
Cover artist: Jim Mooney

FEBRUARY 1963; NO. 312
Cover artists: Dick Dillin, Sheldon Moldoff

MARCH 1963; NO. 313
Cover artist: Sheldon Moldoff

APRIL 1963; NO. 314
Cover artist: Sheldon Moldoff

MAY 1963; NO. 315
Cover artist: Sheldon Moldoff

JUNE 1963; NO. 316
Cover artist: Sheldon Moldoff

JULY 1963; NO. 317
Cover artist: Sheldon Moldoff

SEPTEMBER 1963; NO. 319
Cover artist: Sheldon Moldoff

NOVEMBER 1963; NO. 321
Cover artist: Sheldon Moldoff

DECEMBER 1963; NO. 322
Cover artist: Sheldon Moldoff

JANUARY 1964; NO. 323
Cover artist: Sheldon Moldoff

FEBRUARY 1964; NO. 324
Cover artist: Sheldon Moldoff

MARCH 1964; NO. 325
Cover artist: Sheldon Moldoff

APRIL 1964; NO. 326
Cover artist: Sheldon Moldoff

MAY 1964; NO. 327
Cover artists: Carmine Infantino, Joe Giella

JUNE 1964; NO. 328

Cover artists: Carmine Infantino, Joe Giella

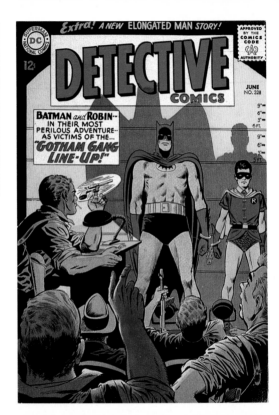

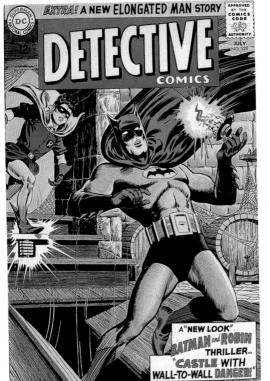

JULY 1964; NO. 329
Cover artists: Carmine Infantino, Murphy Anderson

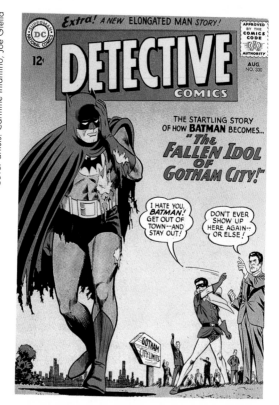

SEPTEMBER 1964; NO. 331
Cover artists: Carmine Infantino, Joe Giella

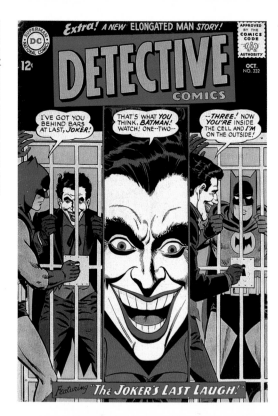

NOVEMBER 1964; NO. 333
Cover artists: Carmine Infantino, Murphy Anderson

JANUARY 1965; NO. 335
Cover artists: Carmine Infantino, Joe Giella

FEBRUARY 1965; NO. 336
Cover artists: Carmine Infantino, Joe Giella

MARCH 1965; NO. 337
Cover artists: Carmine Infantino, Joe Giella

APRIL 1965; NO. 338

Cover artists: Carmine Infantino, Joe Giella

MAY 1965; NO. 339
Cover artists: Carmine Infantino, Joe Giella

JULY 1965; NO. 341
Cover artists: Carmine Infantino, Joe Giella

AUGUST 1965; NO. 342

Cover artists: Carmine Infantino, Joe Giella

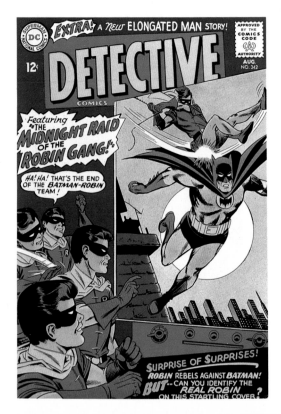

SEPTEMBER 1965; NO. 343
Cover artists: Carmine Infantino, Joe Giella

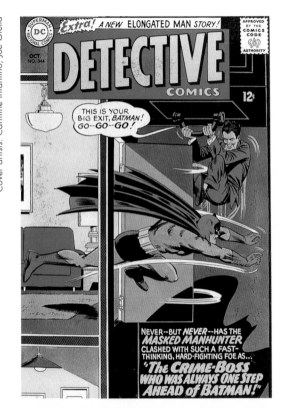

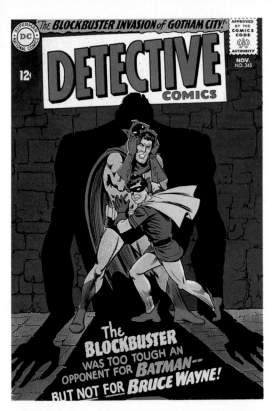

NOVEMBER 1965; NO. 345
Cover artists: Carmine Infantino, Joe Giella

DECEMBER 1965; NO. 346

Cover artists: Carmine Infantino, Joe Giella

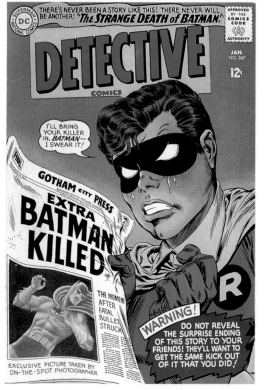

JANUARY 1966; NO. 347
Cover artists: Carmine Infantino, Murphy Anderson

FEBRUARY 1966; NO. 348
Cover artist: Joe Kubert

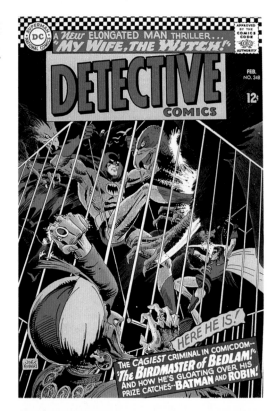

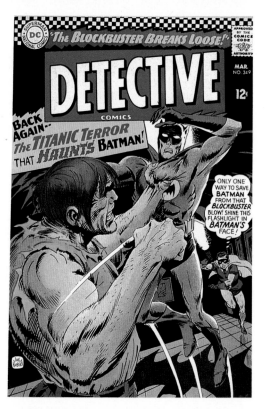

MARCH 1966; NO. 349
Cover artist: Joe Kubert

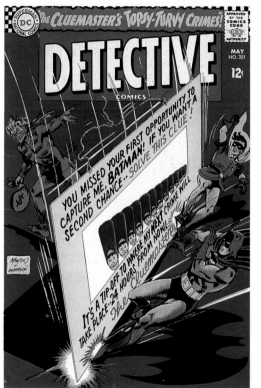

MAY 1966; NO. 351
Cover artists: Carmine Infantino, Murphy Anderson

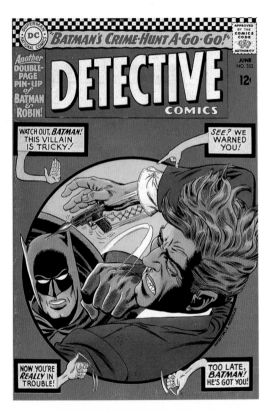

JULY 1966; NO. 353
Cover artists: Carmine Infantino, Joe Giella

AUGUST 1966; NO. 354
Cover artists: Carmine Infantino, Joe Giella

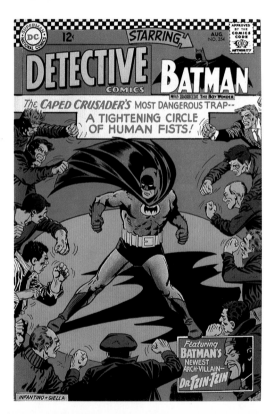

SEPTEMBER 1966; NO. 355
Cover artists: Carmine Infantino, Joe Giella

OCTOBER 1966; NO. 356
Cover artists: Carmine Infantino, Joe Giella

NOVEMBER 1966; NO. 357

Cover artists: Carmine Infantino, Joe Giella

DECEMBER 1966; NO. 358
Cover artists: Carmine Infantino, Joe Giella

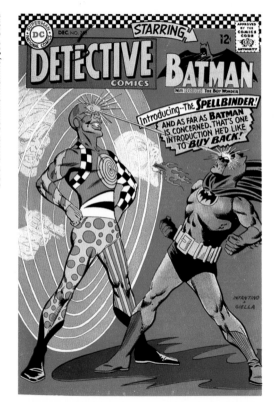

JANUARY 1967; NO. 359
Cover artists: Carmine Infantino, Murphy Anderson

FEBRUARY 1967; NO. 360
Cover artists: Carmine Infantino, Joe Giella

MARCH 1967; NO. 361
Cover artists: Carmine Infantino, Joe Giella

Cover artists: Carmine Infantino, Murphy Anderson

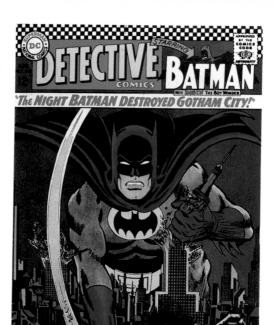

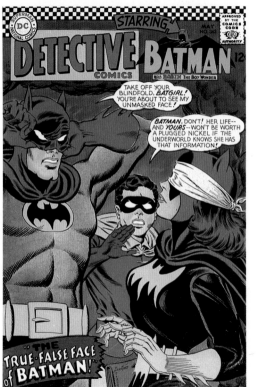

MAY 1967; NO. 363
Cover artists: Carmine Infantino, Murphy Anderson

JUNE 1967; NO. 364

Cover artists: Carmine Infantino, Murphy Anderson

JULY 1967; NO. 365
Cover artists: Carmine Infantino, Murphy Anderson

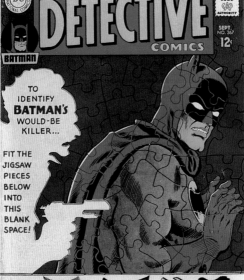

SEPTEMBER 1967; NO. 367
Cover artists: Carmine Infantino, Murphy Anderson

NOVEMBER 1967; NO. 369
Cover artists: Gil Kane, Murphy Anderson

DECEMBER 1967; NO. 370
Cover artists: Carmine Infantino, Neal Adams

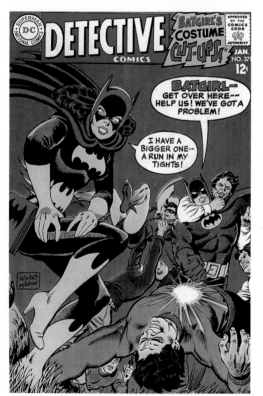

JANUARY 1968: NO. 371
Cover artists: Carmine Infantino, Murphy Anderson

MARCH 1968; NO. 373

Cover artist: Irv Novick

APRIL 1968; NO. 374
Cover artist: Irv Novick

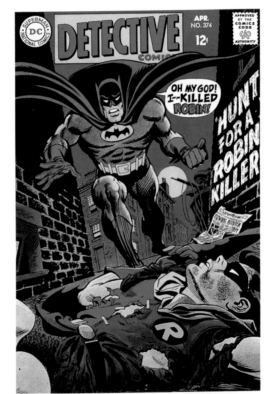

MAY 1968; NO. 375
Cover artist: Irv Novick

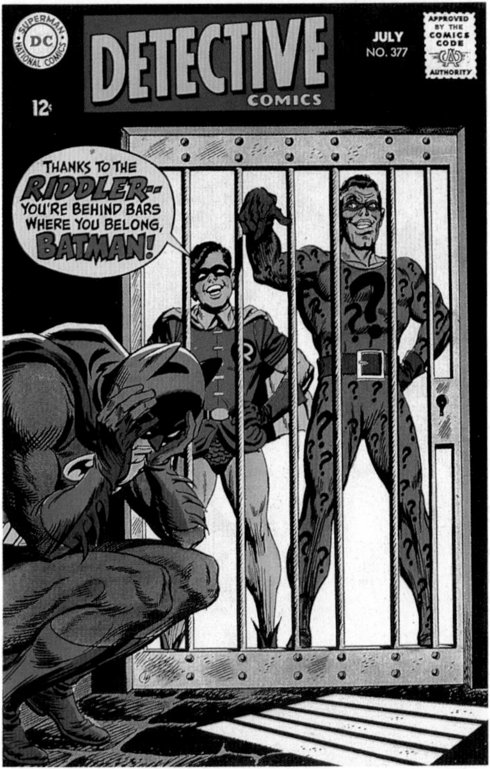

JULY 1968; NO. 377
Cover artist: Irv Novick

SEPTEMBER 1968; NO. 379
Cover artist: Irv Novick

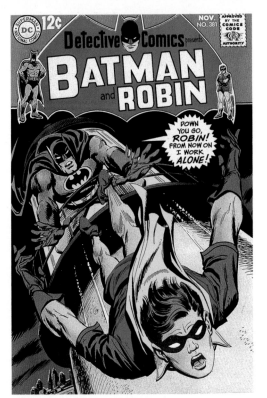

NOVEMBER 1968; NO. 381
Cover artist: Irv Novick

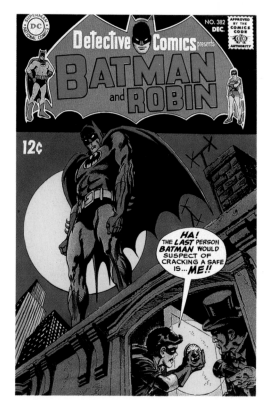

JANUARY 1969; NO. 383
Cover artist: Irv Novick

MARCH 1969; NO. 385
Cover artist: Neal Adams

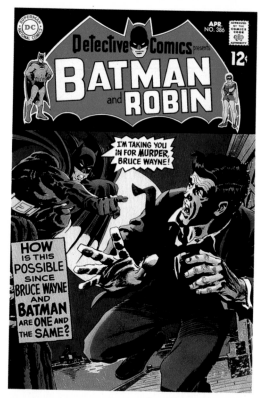

MAY 1969; NO. 387
Cover artist: Irv Novick

JUNE 1969; NO. 388
Cover artist: Irv Novick

JULY 1969; NO. 389
Cover artist: Neal Adams

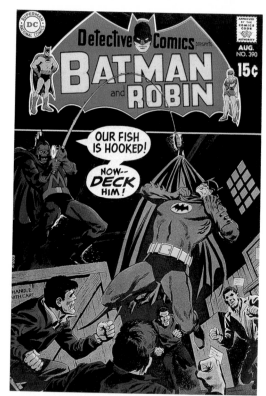

SEPTEMBER 1969; NO. 391
Cover artist: Neal Adams

OCTOBER 1969; NO. 392
Cover artist: Neal Adams

NOVEMBER 1969; NO. 393
Cover artist: Irv Novick

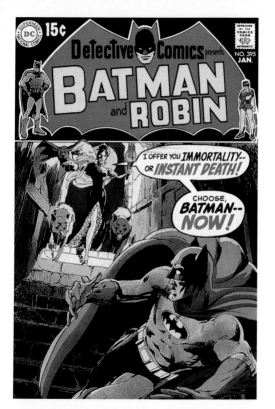

JANUARY 1970; NO. 395
Cover artist: Neal Adams

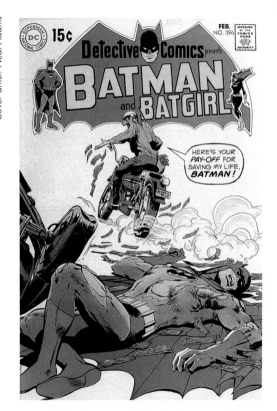

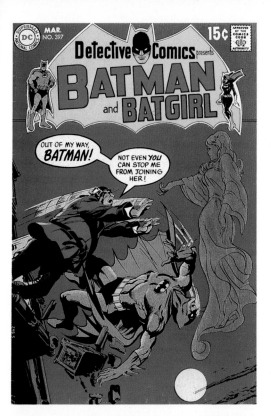

MARCH 1970; NO. 397
Cover artist: Neal Adams

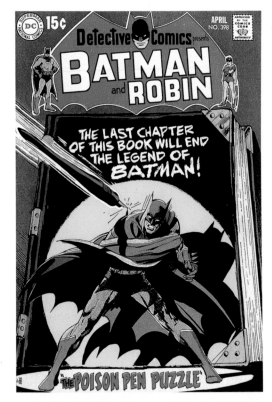

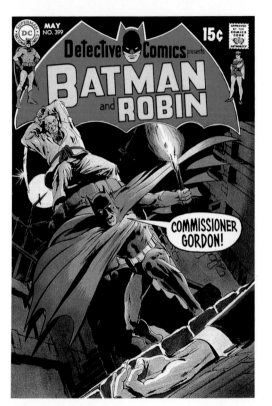

MAY 1970; NO. 399
Cover artist: Neal Adams

JUNE 1970; NO. 400
Cover artist: Neal Adams

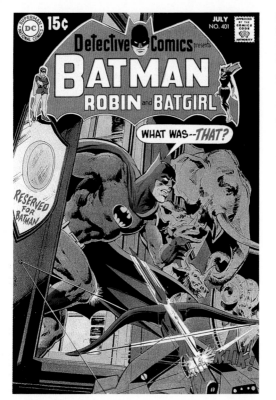

JULY 1970; NO. 401
Cover artists: Neal Adams, Dick Giordano

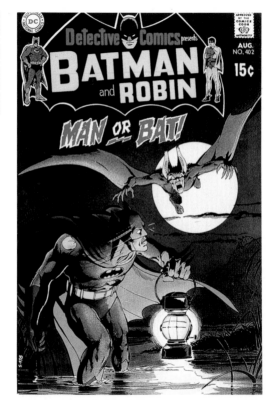

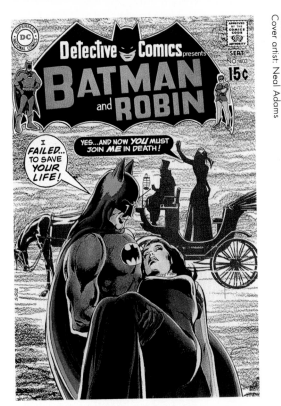

SEPTEMBER 1970; NO. 403
Cover artist: Neal Adams

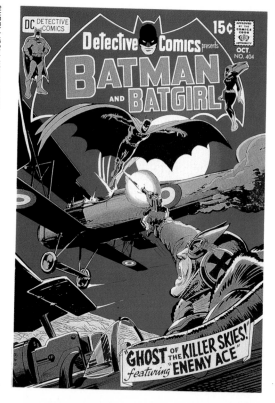

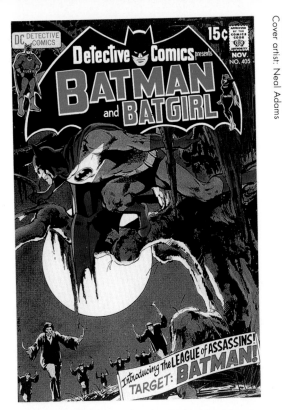

NOVEMBER 1970; NO. 405
Cover artist: Neal Adams

FEBRUARY 1971; NO. 408

Cover artist: Neal Adams

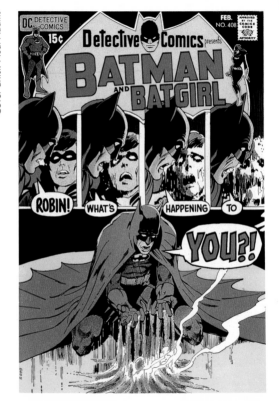

MARCH 1971; NO. 409
Cover artist: Neal Adams

APRIL 1971; NO. 410
Cover artist: Neal Adams

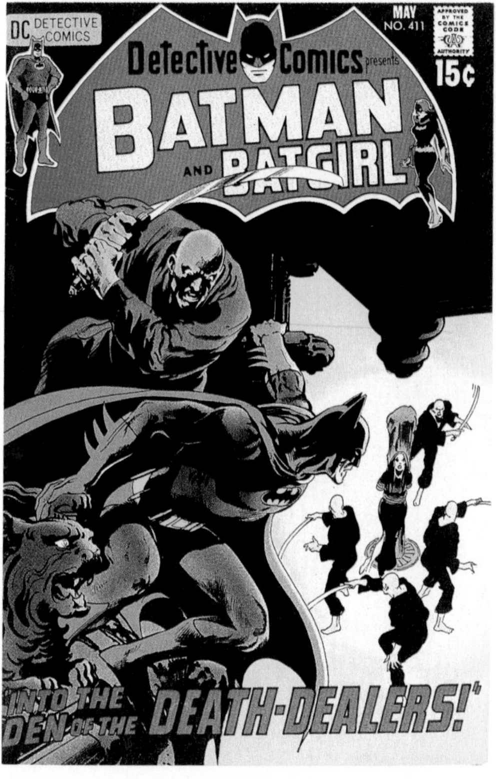

MAY 1971; NO. 411
Cover artist: Neal Adams

JUNE 1971; NO. 412
Cover artist: Neal Adams

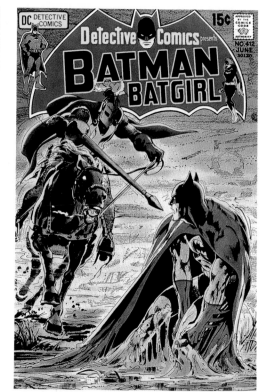

JULY 1971; NO. 413
Cover artist: Neal Adams

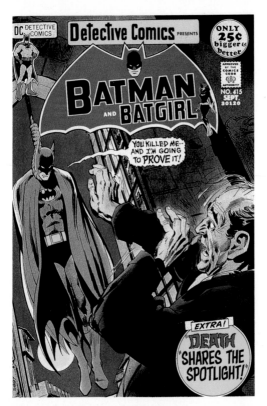

SEPTEMBER 1971; NO. 415

Cover artist: Neal Adams

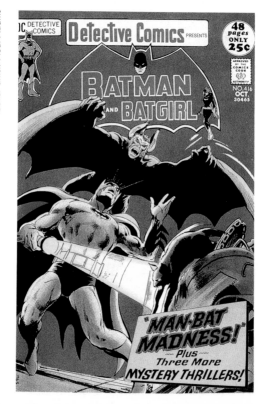

NOVEMBER 1971; NO. 417
Cover artist: Neal Adams

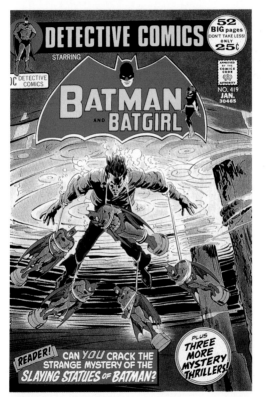

FEBRUARY 1972; NO. 420
Cover artist: Neal Adams

MARCH 1972; NO. 421
Cover artist: Neal Adams

MAY 1972; NO. 423
Cover artist: Mike Kaluta

JUNE 1972; NO. 424
Cover artist: Mike Kaluta

JULY 1972; NO. 425
Cover artist: Bernie Wrighton

SEPTEMBER 1972; NO. 427
Cover artist: Mike Kaluta

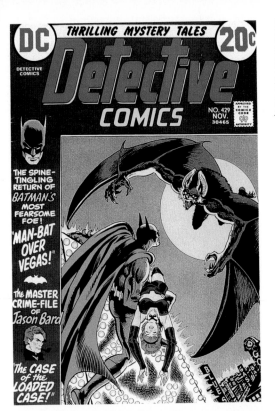

NOVEMBER 1972: NO. 429

Cover artist: Nick Cardy

JANUARY 1973; NO. 431
Cover artist: Mike Kaluta

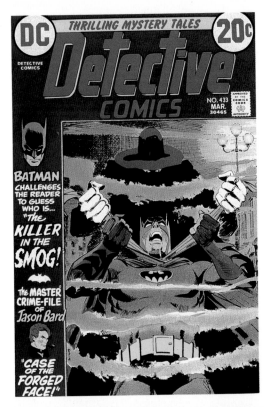

MARCH 1973; NO. 433
Cover artist: Dick Giordano

APRIL 1973; NO. 434
Cover artist: Mike Kaluta

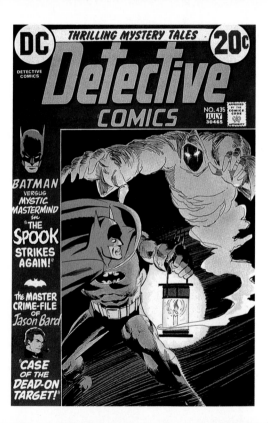

JUNE–JULY 1973; NO. 435
Cover artist: Dick Giordano

AUGUST-SEPTEMBER 1973; NO. 436
Cover artist: Nick Cardy

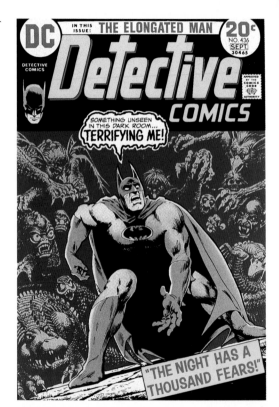

OCTOBER–NOVEMBER 1973; NO. 437

Cover artist: Jim Aparo

DECEMBER 1973–JANUARY 1974; NO. 438
Cover artist: Mike Kaluta

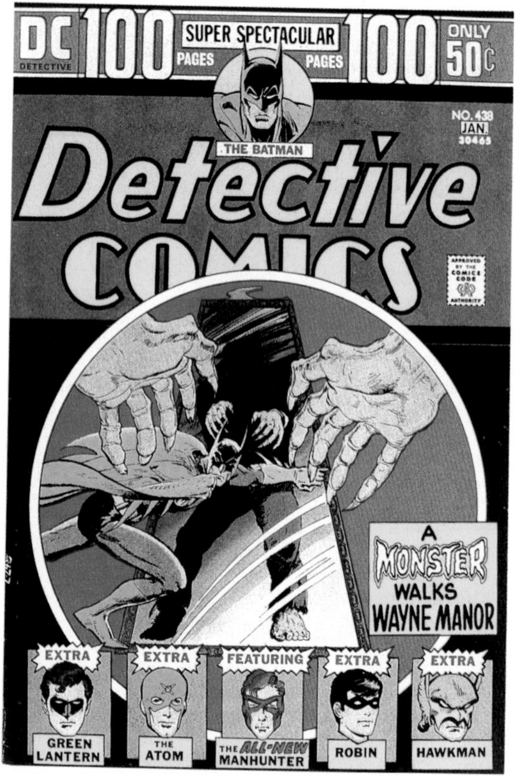

FEBRUARY–MARCH 1974; NO. 439
Cover artist: Neal Adams

JUNE-JULY 1974; NO. 441
Cover artist: Jim Aparo

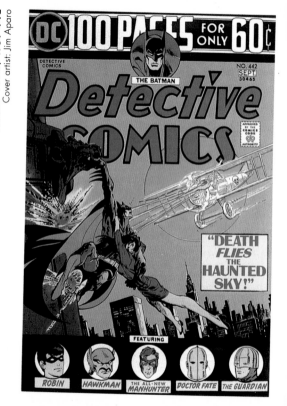

OCTOBER-NOVEMBER 1974; NO. 443
Cover artist: Jim Aparo

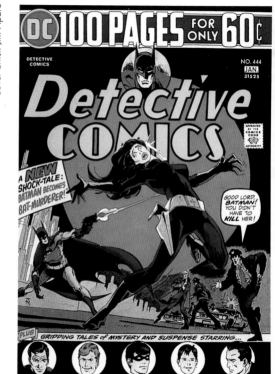

FEBRUARY-MARCH 1975; NO. 445
Cover artist: Jim Aparo

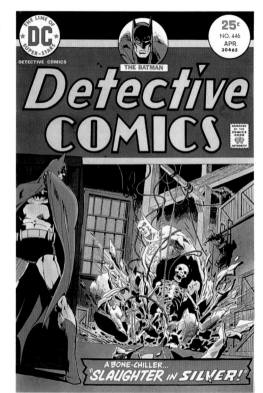

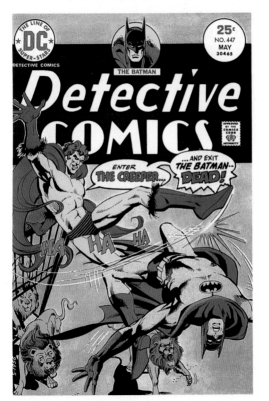

MAY 1975; NO. 447
Cover artist: Dick Giordano

JULY 1975; NO. 449
Cover artist: Ernie Chan

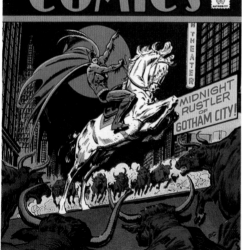

AUGUST 1975; NO. 450
Cover artist: Dick Giordano

SEPTEMBER 1975; NO. 451
Cover artist: Dick Giordano

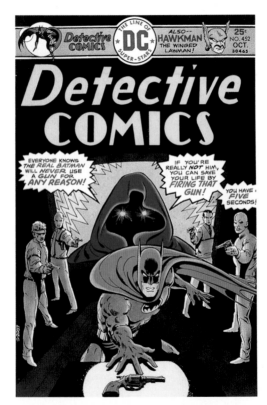

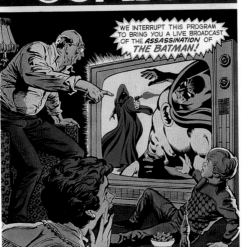

NOVEMBER 1975; NO. 453
Cover artist: Ernie Chan

DECEMBER 1975; NO. 454
Cover artist: Ernie Chan

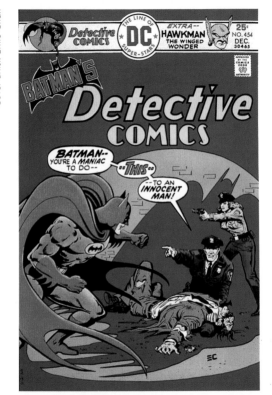

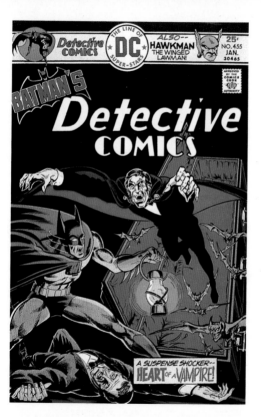

JANUARY 1976; NO. 455

Cover artist: Mike Grell

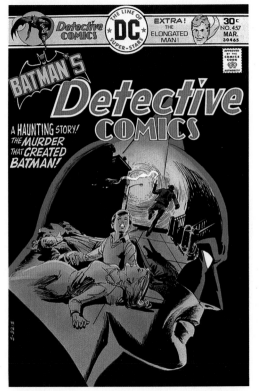

MARCH 1976; NO. 457
Cover artist: Dick Giordano

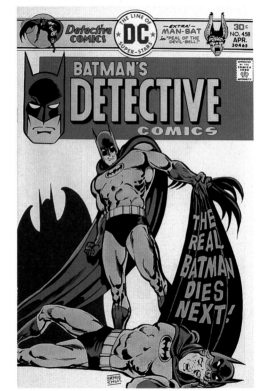

MAY 1976; NO. 459
Cover artist: Ernie Chan

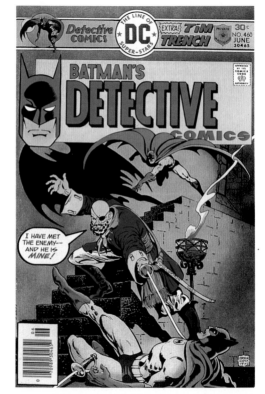

JULY 1976; NO. 461

Cover artist: Ernie Chan

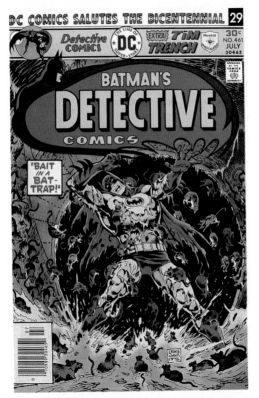

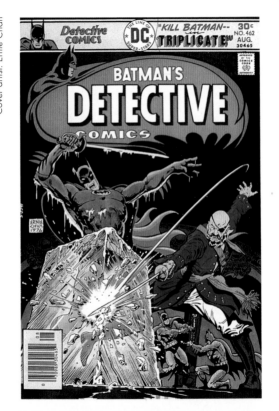

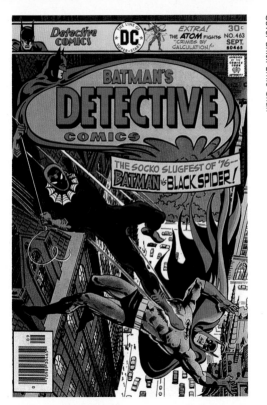

SEPTEMBER 1976; NO. 463

Cover artist: Ernie Chan

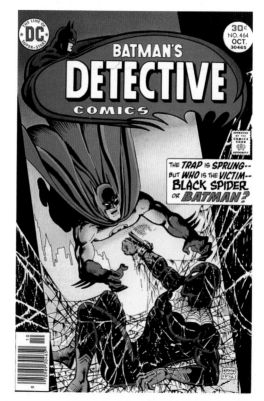

NOVEMBER 1976; NO. 465
Cover artist: Ernie Chan

DECEMBER 1976; NO. 466
Cover artists: Ernie Chan, Vince Colletta

JANUARY-FEBRUARY 1977; NO. 467
Cover artists: Rich Buckler, Vince Colletta

MAY 1977; NO. 469
Cover artist: Jim Aparo

AUGUST 1977; NO. 471
Cover artists: Marshall Rogers, Terry Austin

SEPTEMBER 1977; NO. 472
Cover artists: Marshall Rogers, Terry Austin

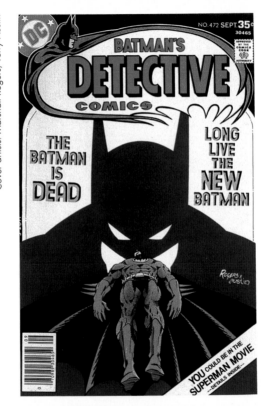

DECEMBER 1977; NO. 474
Cover artists: Marshall Rogers, Terry Austin

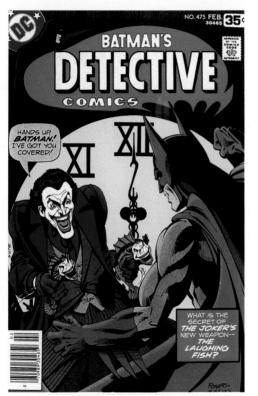

FEBRUARY 1978; NO. 475
Cover artists: Marshall Rogers, Terry Austin

MARCH–APRIL 1978; NO. 476
Cover artists: Marshall Rogers, Terry Austin

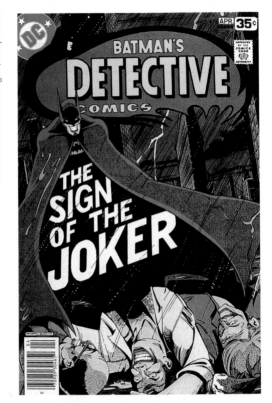

MAY–JUNE 1978; NO. 477
Cover artists: Marshall Rogers, Dick Giordano

SEPTEMBER–OCTOBER 1978; NO. 479
Cover artists: Marshall Rogers, Dick Giordano

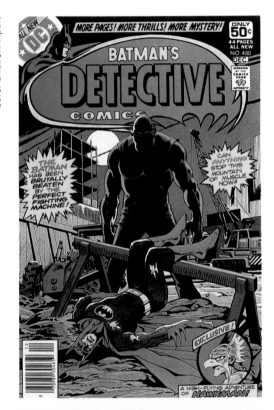

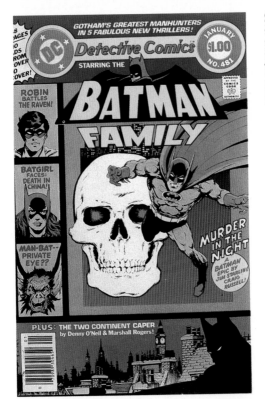

DECEMBER 1978–JANUARY 1979; NO. 481
Cover artist: Jim Starlin

FEBRUARY-MARCH 1979; NO. 482
Cover artists: Rich Buckler, Dick Giordano

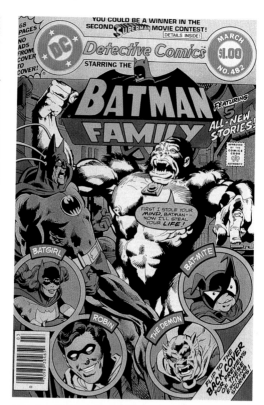

APRIL-MAY 1979; NO. 483
Cover artist: José Luis García-López

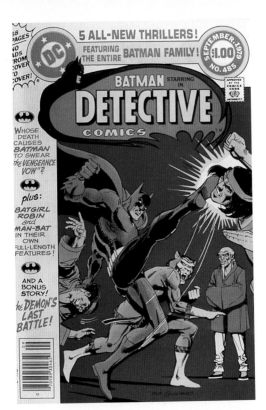

AUGUST-SEPTEMBER 1979; NO. 485
Cover artist: Dick Giordano

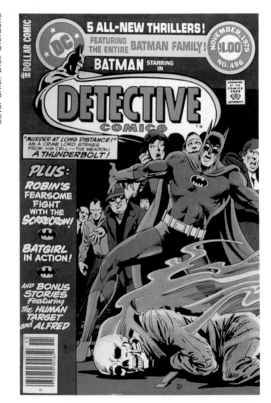

DECEMBER 1979-JANUARY 1980; NO. 487

Cover artist: José Luis García-López

APRIL 1980; NO. 489
Cover artists: Ross Andru, Dick Giordano

JUNE 1980; NO. 491
Cover artists: Ross Andru, Dick Giordano

AUGUST 1980; NO. 493
Cover artist: Jim Aparo

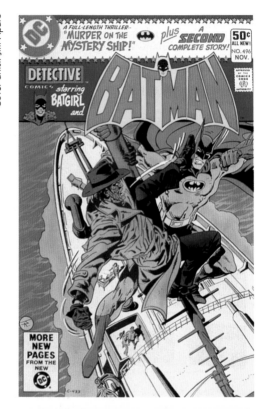

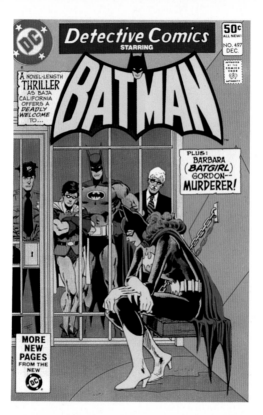

DECEMBER 1980; NO. 497
Cover artist: Jim Aparo

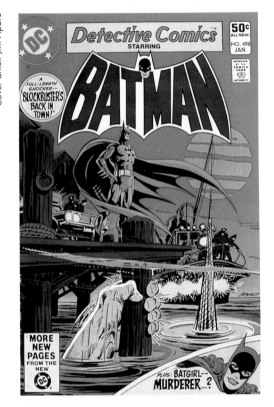

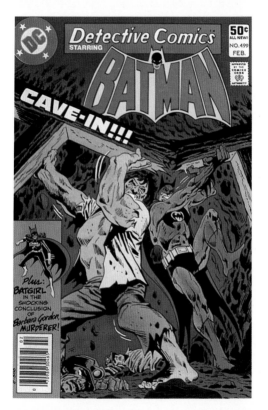

FEBRUARY 1981: NO. 499
Cover artist: Jim Aparo

MARCH 1981; NO. 500

Cover artists: Jim Aparo, José Luis García-López, Dick Giordano, Carmine Infantino, Joe Kubert, Bob LeRose, Walt Simonson, Bob Smith, Tom Yeates

APRIL 1981; NO. 501
Cover artist: Jim Aparo

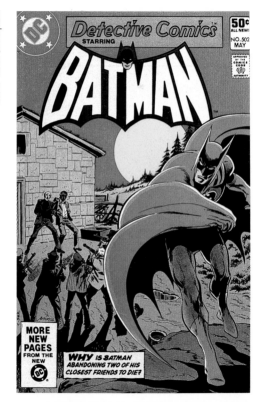

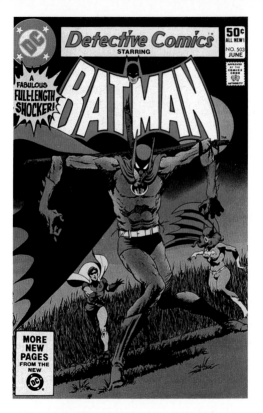

JUNE 1981; NO. 503

Cover artist: Jim Starlin

JULY 1981; NO. 504
Cover artist: Jim Starlin

AUGUST 1981; NO. 505
Cover artists: Rich Buckler, Dick Giordano

SEPTEMBER 1981; NO. 506
Cover artists: Rich Buckler, Dick Giordano

OCTOBER 1981; NO. 507
Cover artists: Denys Cowan, Dick Giordano

DECEMBER 1981; NO. 509
Cover artist: Jim Aparo

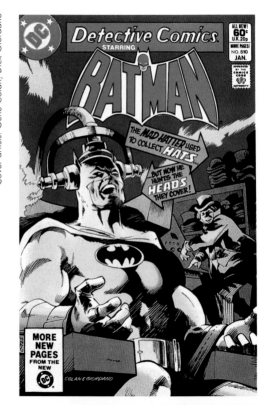

JANUARY 1982; NO. 510
Cover artists: Gene Colan, Dick Giordano

FEBRUARY 1982; NO. 511
Cover artists: Rich Buckler, Dick Giordano

MARCH 1982; NO. 512

Cover artists: Gene Colan, Dick Giordano

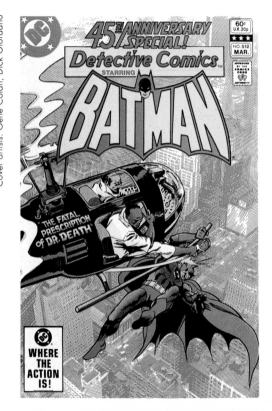

APRIL 1982; NO. 513
Cover artists: Rich Buckler, Dick Giordano

MAY 1982; NO. 514

Cover artists: Don Newton, Dick Giordano

JUNE 1982; NO. 515
Cover artists: Ross Andru, Dick Giordano

JULY 1982; NO. 516
Cover artists: Ross Andru, Dick Giordano

AUGUST 1982; NO. 517
Cover artists: Gene Colan, Frank Giacoia

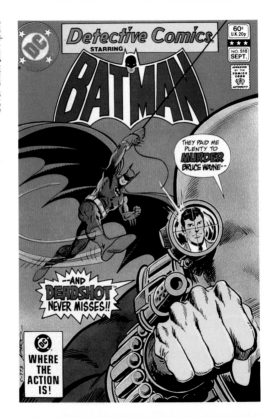

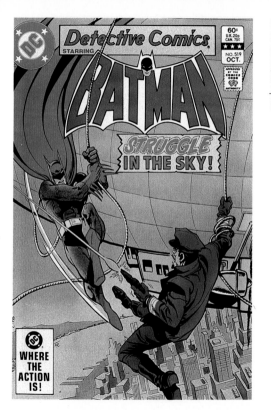

OCTOBER 1982; NO. 519
Cover artist: Jim Aparo

DECEMBER 1982; NO. 521
Cover artist: Jim Aparo

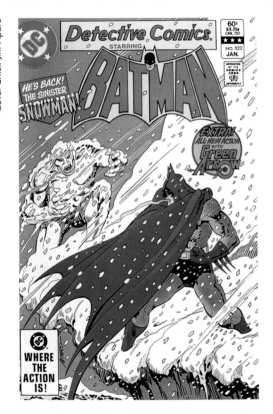

FEBRUARY 1983; NO. 523
Cover artists: Ed Hannigan, Dick Giordano

APRIL 1983; NO. 525
Cover artists: Ed Hannigan, Dick Giordano

MAY 1983; NO. 526
Cover artists: Don Newton, Dick Giordano

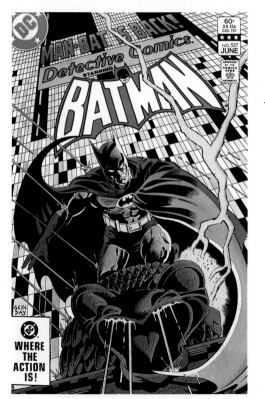

JUNE 1983; NO. 527
Cover artist: Gene Day

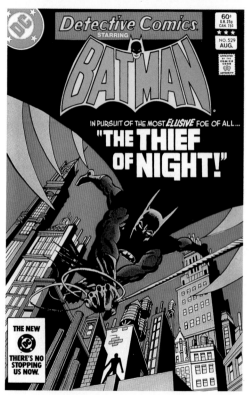

AUGUST 1983; NO. 529
Cover artists: Ed Hannigan, Dick Giordano

SEPTEMBER 1983; NO. 530
Cover artists: Gene Colan, Dick Giordano

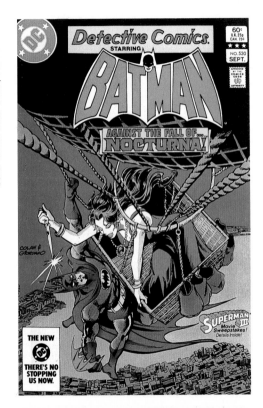

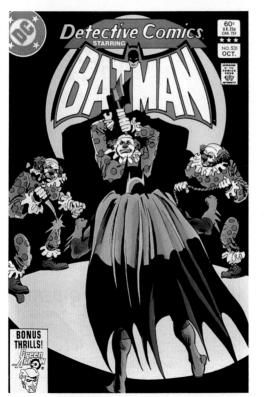

OCTOBER 1983; NO. 531
Cover artists: Gene Colan, Dick Giordano

NOVEMBER 1983; NO. 532
Cover artists: Gene Colan, Dick Giordano

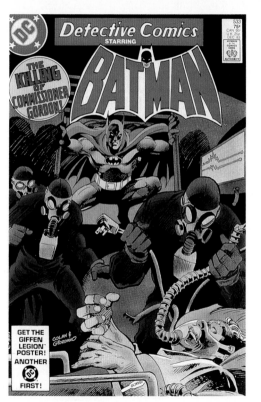

DECEMBER 1983; NO. 533
Cover artists: Gene Colan, Dick Giordano

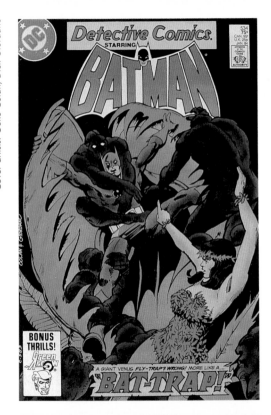

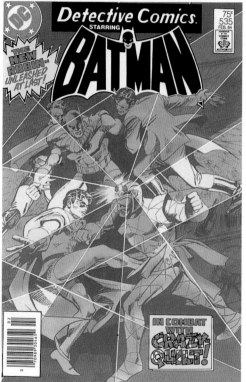

FEBRUARY 1984; NO. 535
Cover artists: Gene Colan, Dick Giordano

MARCH 1984; NO. 536
Cover artists: Paris Cullins, Dick Giordano

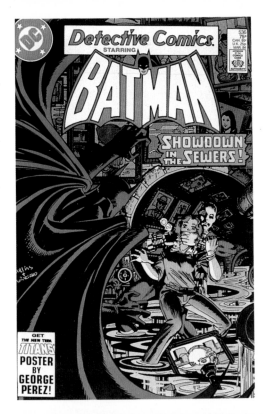

APRIL 1984; NO. 537
Cover artists: Gene Colan, Dick Giordano

JUNE 1984; NO. 539

Cover artists: Ed Hannigan, Dick Giordano

JULY 1984; NO. 540

Cover artists: Gene Colan, Dick Giordano

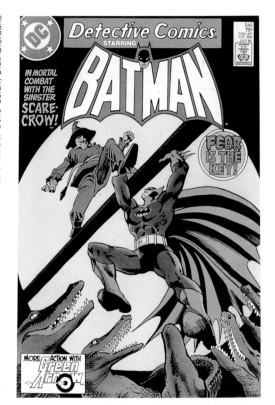

AUGUST 1984; NO. 541
Cover artists: Gene Colan, Dick Giordano

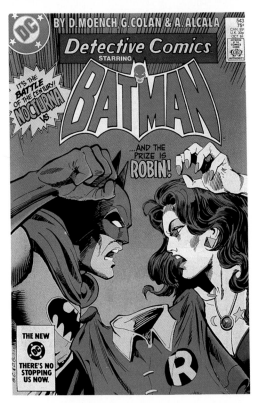

OCTOBER 1984; NO. 543
Cover artists: Gene Colan, Dick Giordano

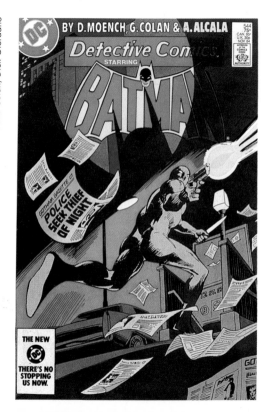

DECEMBER 1984; NO. 545
Cover artists: Gene Colan, Dick Giordano

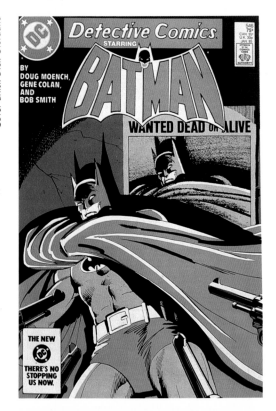

FEBRUARY 1985; NO. 547
Cover artists: Pat Broderick, Romeo Tanghal

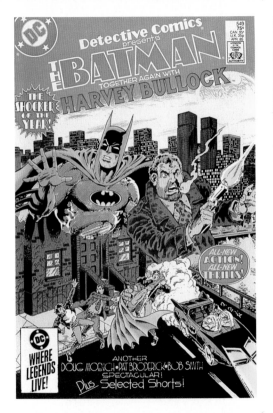

MAY 1985; NO. 550
Cover artist: Pat Broderick

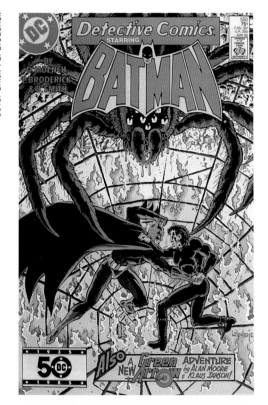

JUNE 1985; NO. 551
Cover artist: Pat Broderick

JULY 1985; NO. 552
Cover artist: Pat Broderick

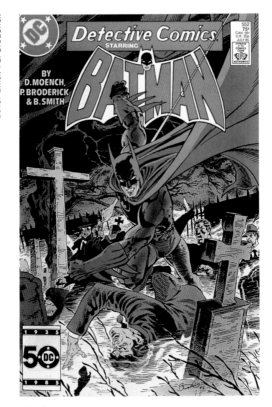

AUGUST 1985; NO. 553
Cover artist: Klaus Janson

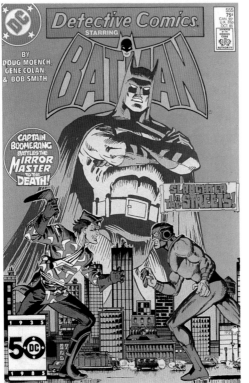

OCTOBER 1985; NO. 555
Cover artists: Paris Cullins, Dick Giordano

DECEMBER 1985; NO. 557
Cover artists: Gene Colan, Dick Giordano

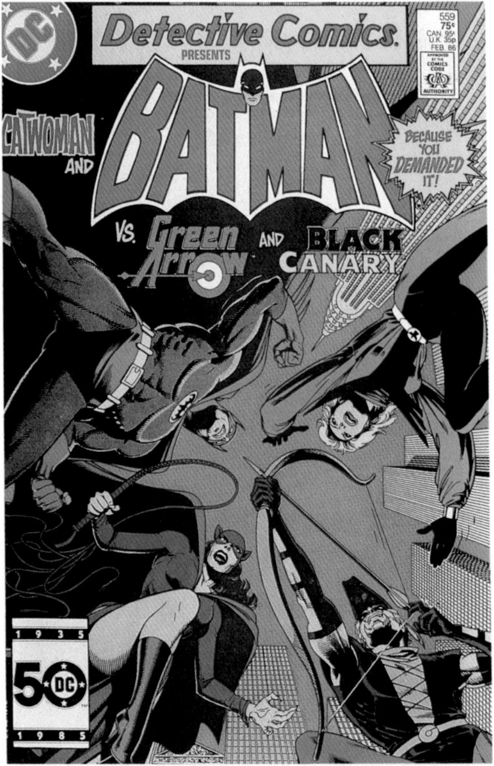

FEBRUARY 1986; NO. 559
Cover artist: Brian Bolland

MARCH 1986; NO. 560
Cover artists: Gene Colan, Dick Giordano

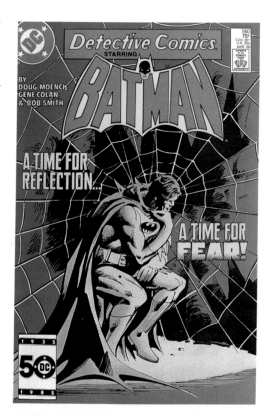

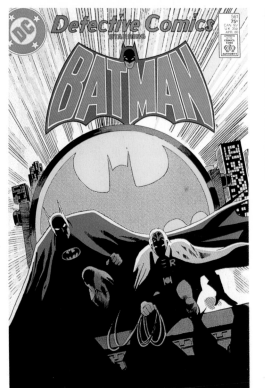

APRIL 1986; NO. 561
Cover artists: Gene Colan, Dick Giordano

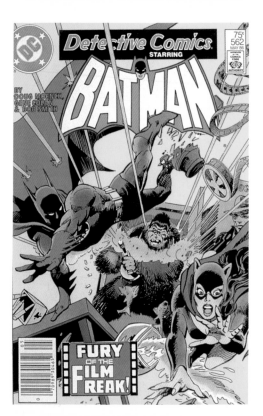

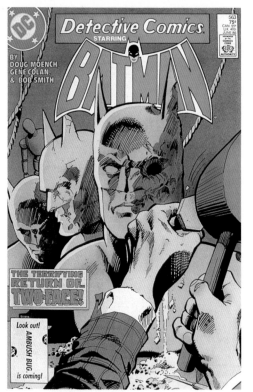

JUNE 1986; NO. 563
Cover artists: Gene Colan, Dick Giordano

JULY 1986; NO. 564

Cover artists: Gene Colan, Dick Giordano

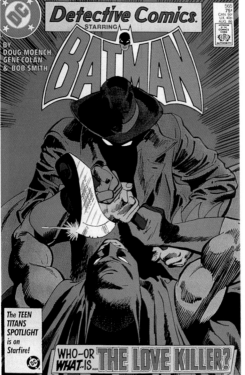

AUGUST 1986; NO. 565
Cover artists: Gene Colan, Dick Giordano

SEPTEMBER 1986; NO. 566
Cover artist: Dick Giordano

OCTOBER 1986; NO. 567
Cover artist: Klaus Janson

NOVEMBER 1986; NO. 568
Cover artist: Klaus Janson

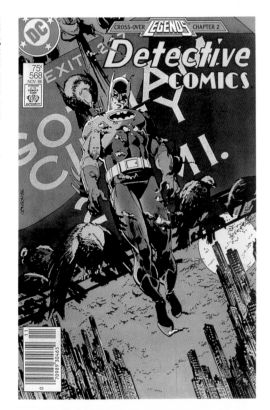

DECEMBER 1986; NO. 569
Cover artists: Alan Davis, Paul Neary

FEBRUARY 1987; NO. 571
Cover artist: Alan Davis

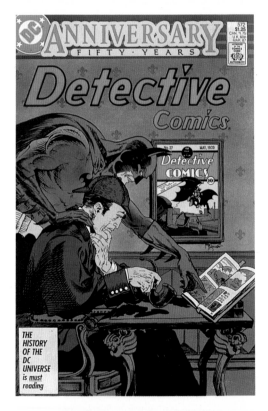

APRIL 1987; NO. 573
Cover artists: Alan Davis, Paul Neary

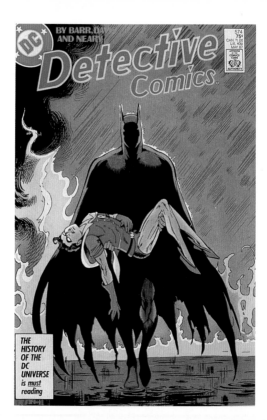

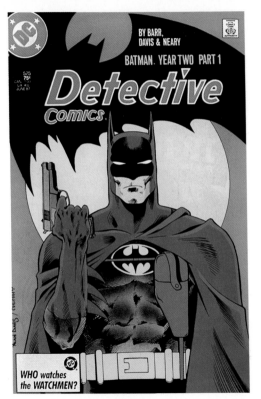

JUNE 1987; NO. 575
Cover artists: Alan Davis, Paul Neary

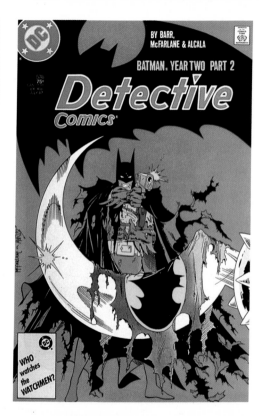

AUGUST 1987; NO. 577

Cover artists: Todd McFarlane, Pablo Marcos

SEPTEMBER 1987; NO. 578
Cover artists: Todd McFarlane, Pablo Marcos

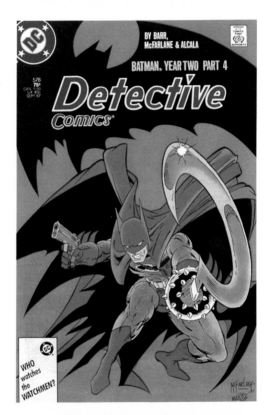

OCTOBER 1987; NO. 579
Cover artist: Norm Breyfogle

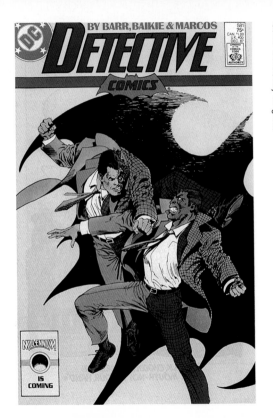

DECEMBER 1987; NO. 581
Cover artist: Jerry Bingham

JANUARY 1988; NO. 582
Cover artist: Jerry Bingham

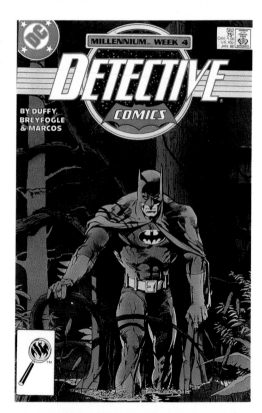

FEBRUARY 1988; NO. 583

Cover artist: Mike Mignola

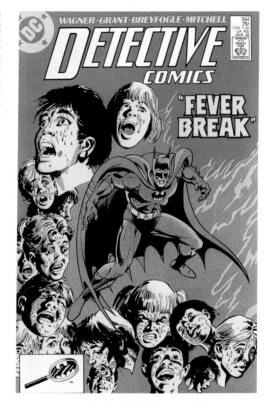

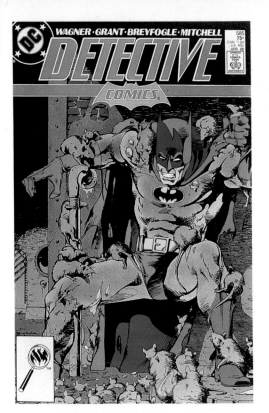

APRIL 1988; NO. 585

Cover artist: Jerry Bingham

JUNE 1988; NO. 587
Cover artist: Norm Breyfogle

JULY 1988; NO. 588
Cover artist: Norm Breyfogle

AUGUST 1988; NO. 589

Cover artist: Norm Breyfogle

SEPTEMBER 1988; NO. 590
Cover artist: Norm Breyfogle

OCTOBER 1988; NO. 591
Cover artist: Norm Breyfogle

NOVEMBER 1988; NO. 592
Cover artist: Norm Breyfogle

DECEMBER 1988; NO. 593
Cover artist: Norm Breyfogle

1988; NO. 594

Cover artist: Norm Breyfogle

1988; NO. 595
Cover artists: Paris Cullins, Malcolm Jones III

JANUARY 1989; NO. 596
Cover artist: Norm Breyfogle

FEBRUARY 1989; NO. 597
Cover artist: Norm Breyfogle

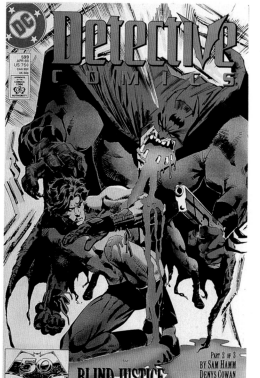

APRIL 1989; NO. 599

Cover artists: Denys Cowan, Malcolm Jones III

MAY 1989; NO. 600

Cover artists: Denys Cowan, Malcolm Jones III